ACTIVE SHOOTER

ACTIVE SHOOTER

The Greatest Threat to American Citizens...
How to Identify, React and Defend Yourself
and Family During an Active Shooter Event

BY FRANK MITCHELL

Copyright © 2017 by Frank Mitchell, FamilySurvival.com & 5280 Publishing, LLC

All rights reserved. This book or any portion thereof may not be reproduced or used in any manner whatsoever without the express written permission of the publisher except for the use of brief quotations in a book review.

Printed in the United States of America

First Printing, 2017

ISBN 978-0-9974376-8-3

5280 Publishing, LLC dba FamilySurvival.com
453 E. Wonderview Ave.
Estes Park, CO 80517
www.FamilySurvival.com

DISCLAIMER OF LIABILITY AND WARRANTY

This publication describes the author's opinions regarding the subject matter herein. The author and publisher are not rendering advice or services pertaining to specific individuals or situations. For specific advice, or if expert assistance is required, the services of a qualified professional should be obtained. The author and publisher assume no responsibility whatsoever for the use of the information in this publication or for decisions made or actions taken based, in whole or in part, on the information in this publication. The author and publisher make no warranties, express or implied, regarding the information. Without limiting the foregoing, the author and publisher specifically disclaim and will not be responsible for any liability, loss, or risk incurred directly, indirectly or incidentally as a consequence of the use or misuse of any advice or information presented herein. Use this publication and information with good judgment and do the best you can in your particular situation.

You agree to indemnify and hold the author and publisher, and their respective officers, directors, agents, employees, contractors and suppliers, harmless from any claim or demand, including reasonable attorneys' fees, related to your use or misuse of this publication or the information contained therein. You further agree that you will cooperate fully in the defense of any such claims.

Notice: As the purchaser of this publication you are permitted to store it and print it for your own personal use only. Otherwise, no part of this publication may be reproduced, stored in a retrieval system or transmitted in any form or by any means, electronic, mechanical, photocopying, recording, or otherwise without the prior written permission of the copyright owner and publisher. It is illegal to make a copy of all or part of this publication for someone else, even if you do not charge for the copy. If you have purchased this book from anywhere other than FamilySurvival.com, including eBay, please report it to support@familysurvival.support immediately.

COPYRIGHT

Those who have received or purchased the guide are neither authorized nor permitted to transmit copies of this guide to anyone without written permission. Giving away copies to people who haven't paid for them is illegal under international copyright laws and will submit you to possible legal action. Therefore, the utilization of this material is limited to personal use only.

TERMS AND DISCLAIMER

By using, viewing, and interacting with this guide or the FamilySurvival.com website, you agree to all terms of engagement, thus assuming complete responsibility for your own actions.

The authors and publishers will not be held liable or claim accountability for any loss or injuries. Use, view, and interact with these resources at your own risk. All publications from FamilySurvival.com and its related companies are strictly for informational purposes only.

While all attempts have been made to verify the accuracy of information provided on our website and within our publications, neither the authors nor the publishers are responsible for assuming liability for possible inaccuracies. The authors and publishers disclaim any responsibility for the inaccuracy of the content, including but not limited to errors or omissions. Loss of property, injury to self or others, and even death could occur as a direct or indirect consequence of the use and application of any content found herein.

YOU SETTLE INTO YOUR SEAT AND ENJOY the premiere of the latest Hollywood blockbuster. The action is thrilling, the cinematography is breathtaking. Out of the corner of your eye, a figure emerges from one of the fire exits. Curiously, the fire alarm doesn't sound. He's dressed in a peculiar fashion; he's got body armor on as well as some sort of armored leggings and a gas mask. He carries what appears to be a couple of weapons. You think to yourself – "that's a great costume" – because many other people in the audience are dressed the same way. The figure then reaches for a smoke canister and pops it off, causing smoke to billow out and your eyes to water. The last thing you remember is coughing on acrid smoke while gunshots ring out....

Another time, another place. You're seated in the classroom of your college while the professor drones on and on. Twenty minutes till the class ends – can't wait for the weekend. The classroom door opens a crack, and an Asian student peeks, in surveys the classroom, and then closes the door. It happens so quickly that the professor doesn't notice. You say to yourself – "he's probably lost". You go back to listening to the lecture. Ten minutes to go. Suddenly, the door opens again, and the same

Asian student peeks in – this time, he takes a longer look. The professor notices, and asks the student if he's lost – the student doesn't answer, only shuts the door. Weird - it's the middle of April, not the beginning of September. How could anyone be lost so late in the school year? You go back to daydreaming, and check your watch. You're about to doze off as you hear a popping noise down the hallway...wait – that sounds like gunfire....

* * *

The above two scenarios represent fictional representations of real events that actually occurred – the first one was the Aurora Theater shooting of 2012, in which James Eagan Holmes stormed a packed theater, set off a tear gas canister, and began shooting, killing 12 people and wounding 58 others. The second scenario is the Virginia Tech Massacre of 2007, in which Seung-Hui Cho killed 32 people and injured 23 others while on a shooting spree at his college. In both of these cases, the perpetrators were labeled as *Active Shooters*, a term far too familiar to the American public today.

An active shooter can strike any place, at any time. They have struck restaurants, post offices, schools, theaters, shopping malls, and just about anywhere else you can think of. Their methods of operation are simple – in a nutshell, the active shooter seeks to trap as many victims within a contained area as possible, an area in which it's almost guaranteed that the victims will be unarmed. The shooter isn't looking for a ransom or hostages – he is looking for a high body count. Because of the tactics active shooters use, they are usually very successful in their mission, and thankfully, they don't often get to try it again as an active shooter incident usually ends with either the suicide of the shooter, his death at the hands of police, or his capture.

It might seem on the outset that it's almost impossible to survive an active shooter event. While there are definitely some unwinnable circumstances that victims find themselves in, realize that for every victim, *there are many times more survivors*. It is possible to survive an active shooter event – and even avoid one in the first place. Additionally, realize that the body count on active shooter events is relatively low compared to what it *could be*. While an active shooter event that results in death is an awful tragedy, active shooters are rarely efficient in terms of deaths per round of ammunition fired, which is another facet of these events to consider. Keep in mind that:

- Even though most active shooter events result in what is perceived as a high body count (i.e. Virginia Tech's 33 dead), consider that the shooter had over *400 rounds of ammunition* on his person, and expended some 200 rounds!
- Even densely populated venues such as the Aurora Theater shooting are survivable. There were *hundreds* of people in that theater, conveniently sitting mere inches apart. It should have been like shooting fish in a barrel, yet only *12 people* died.
- Active shooter events are often precipitated by a *single*, highly vulnerable person.
- Police tactics have changed to provide the most efficient response to an active shooter, meaning that you're most likely to receive a police response within minutes of such an event.

Take heart. An active shooter event is a traumatic, deadly scenario that no one wants to be caught in the middle of. You can, however, survive such an event if you know a thing or two about how these sorts of incidents normally go down – and *how survivors made it out alive*.

A BRIEF NOTE:

This manual starts with the supposition that if you happen to find yourself in the midst of an active shooter scenario, you will most likely be *unarmed*. This is an incredibly important distinction to make. There are several reasons why we chose to present this manual as such:

- Many states still have draconian prohibitions on concealed carry by normal citizens, so you may not be able to carry in the first place.
- While an armed response to an active shooter is optimal, your family members, such as your husband, wife, or children may not be armed. They still need to know how to respond to such an event.
- You won't be able to be legally armed in some venues. Areas like courtrooms, federal buildings, and sterile areas of airports are areas in which even legally carrying citizens may not enter. Such areas are magnets for active shooters – because they *know* everyone will be unarmed.
- Simply being armed is not the panacea for a response to an active shooter. While being armed is a definite benefit, it will not necessarily guarantee survival.

ACTIVE SHOOTER EVENTS – A BRIEF HISTORY

The concept of a single armed individual entering an area where many unarmed and innocent people were congregating, then shooting up the place for maximum effect, is not a new one. Active shooters, although they were not always referred to as such, have been slaughtering innocent people for over a century. They all have extremely common methods they use and the results of their heinous actions are usually the same – the death of innocents. What are these common traits? Did the shooters compare notes or study each others crimes to better perfect their killing? How did the survivors make it out? What caused the death of the shooter? All these questions and more can be answered by looking at several of the higher profile shootings, and comparing them. If knowledge is power, then knowing what exactly happened in these events is the *key* to survival.

The active shooter events profiled below represent some of the worst active shooter events to happen within the last 25 years:

SAN YSIDRO MCDONALD'S SHOOTING:

When: July 18, 1984
Where: McDonald's Restaurant, San Ysidro, CA
Active Shooter: 1 – James Huberty
Fate of active shooter: Death by police sniper
Approximate number of persons present: unknown
Number of deaths: 21
Number of injured: 19
Approximate duration of event: 77 minutes
Gun Free Zone? Yes, California had no provision for lawful citizen carry at the time.

What happened: Disgruntled gunman James Huberty entered a busy McDonald's restaurant and indiscriminately shot patrons, expending a staggering 257 rounds of ammunition. Victims ranged from 8 months old to 77 years. Due to police tactics at the time, Huberty was able to keep shooting people, unmolested.

What worked for survivors: Taking refuge in a barricaded room away from the shooter.

What didn't work: Police tactics at the time, which called for a cordon around the area. This allowed Huberty to kill people at will without being bothered by police.

LUBY'S CAFETERIA MASSACRE:

When: October 16, 1991
Where: Luby's Cafeteria, Killeen, TX
Active Shooter: 1 - George Hennard
Fate of active shooter: Death by suicide
Approximate number of persons present: 80
Number of deaths: 23
Number inured: 20
Approximate duration of event: 16 minutes
Gun Free Zone? Yes, Texas law at the time prevented citizens from carrying concealed.

What happened: Gunman George Hennard drove his pickup truck through the front window of Luby's Cafeteria, a busy restaurant, at the *peak of the lunch hour rush.* He emerged from the vehicle and started shooting patrons. All attempts to subdue him by patrons were unsuccessful. Some patrons escaped the kill zone when another patron threw himself through a plate glass window, creating a method of egress. Hennard systematically stalked and shot as many people as he could, finally shooting himself.

What worked for survivors: Creating an exit where there was none.

What didn't work: Playing dead – Hennard walked the restaurant, systematically shooting everyone to ensure they were dead.

by Frank Mitchell

COLUMBINE HIGH SCHOOL SHOOTING:

When: April 20, 1999
Where: Columbine High School, Columbine, CO
Active Shooter: 2 – Eric Harris, Dylan Klebold
Fate of active shooter: Death by suicide
Approximate number of persons present: hundreds
Number of deaths: 13
Number inured: 21
Approximate duration of event: approximately 49 minutes
Gun Free Zone? Yes

What happened: Klebold and Harris, armed with a variety of small arms and improvised explosive devices, stormed their high school. Initially, they had planted a couple of propane bombs within the cafeteria, and then the pair retreated outside to await the explosions, which never happened since the bombs failed to detonate. They then decided to charge the school, and killed a number of students indiscriminately. Most of their shots while proceeding down school hallways missed their intended targets. They then entered the school library, which was full of students who were hiding under desks and other furniture – Klebold And Harris were able to kill many by simply shooting under desks.

What worked for survivors: Fleeing the premises immediately.

What didn't work: Hiding in place – many victims were easily discovered and shot. Also, police set up a cordon that simply allowed the shooters to kill more people.

VIRGINIA TECH MASSACRE

When: April 16, 2007
Where: Virginia Tech University, Blacksburg, VA
Active Shooter: 1- Seng-Hui Cho
Fate of active shooter: Death by suicide
Approximate number of persons present: hundreds
Number of deaths: 32
Number inured: 23
Approximate duration of event: approximately 20 minutes, two separate events, two hours apart
Gun Free Zone? Yes

What happened: The shooter, Cho, killed his first victims in a dorm room before returning to his own dorm room, where he changes his clothes. This distracted first responders, who were occupied with the first shootings. Cho then moved to a different part of the campus, he entered Norris Hall, chaining the three main entrance doors shut, and then initiated a systematic massacre. Cho went from room to room, shooting as he went – in some cases, he was denied entry into some of the classrooms by students who had barricaded the doors shut. He circled back to some of the rooms, killing even more people. Finally, he shot himself in the head, having expended hundreds of rounds of ammunition.

What worked for survivors: Escaping, barricading themselves inside of rooms, playing dead.

What didn't work: Some people within barricaded rooms were shot through the door because they were standing behind the barricade.

AURORA THEATER SHOOTING

When: July 20, 2012
Where: Century 16 Multiplex, Aurora, CO
Active Shooter: 1- James Holmes
Fate of active shooter: Capture by police
Approximate number of persons present: hundreds
Number of deaths: 12
Number inured: 58
Approximate duration of event: approximately 10 minutes
Gun Free Zone? Yes.

What happened: Holmes, the shooter, purchased a ticket to view the premiere of a massive Hollywood blockbuster's midnight screening. He sat through the movie for approximately 20 minutes, and then exited the theater through an emergency exit door which he had propped open earlier. The alarm failed to sound. He went to his vehicle, where he changed clothes and donned a bulletproof vest, bulletproof leggings, and picked up his weapons. He reentered the theater through the same door, deployed a tear gas canister, and began shooting audience members indiscriminately. Initially, audience members thought that he was part of the promotion of the film since other audience members were also in costume. He was later captured without incident by police as he returned to his car.

What worked for survivors: Escape, hiding behind theater seats.

What didn't: Waiting to confirm whether the shooter was in fact a threat, or just part of the show.

THE SUMMARY

First, before we jump to conclusions about the efficacy of methods to avoid an active shooter, we must keep a few things in mind. First, the shooter cases profiled above are only a *small sampling* of active shooter events. Many others have been left out due to brevity. Second, the examples used are large, mass shootings. Keep in mind that an active shooter can kill only a single person, and that person could be *you*. The number of victims doesn't make the event any less dangerous.

Active shooter incidents all have certain hallmarks, certain distinctive features that most of them share. In this aspect, they are unlike other crimes of passion which seemingly have no rhyme or reason. Knowing what these traits are will help you understand the nature of these events, and better plan for them. Consider that in the bulk of American mass casualty active shooter events, the following precepts were found to be true:

Planning: Most all of the active shooter events profiled included heavy planning on the part of the shooter. Huberty (San Ysidro McDonald's) scoped out two other locations before deciding that the McDonalds' restaurant would reap more victims. Klebold and Harris (Columbine) attended the high school they attacked, and thus were intimately familiar with the layout of the facility. Additionally, they each practiced extensively with the weapons they used to perpetrate the massacre, and made detailed plans of how they were going to carry it out, including creating a diversionary explosion nearly a mile away. Cho, (Virginia Tech) had the presence of mind to chain the main exit doors to ensure victims could not escape. Holmes (Aurora Theater) scouted the inside of the theater before the shooting, and propped the exit door open. Nidal Malik Hassan, who perpetrated the Fort

Hood shooting, extensively practiced marksmanship before the shooting, and equipped his pistol with a red laser sight to aid in target acquisition. Anders Breivik, the Norway active shooter who killed 77 persons, not only set up a diversionary attack, but also extensively used disguises to fool his victims into thinking he was a police officer.

The point is, an active shooter incident is not something that is a crime of passion. While there were some incidents in which a workplace altercation occurred and then the shooter went home and got guns, coming back and shooting his victims, most active shooter events of significant scale are carefully planned events in which the shooter *knows the layout of the building or terrain*.

Deadliness: Believe it or not, most active shooter events are not especially effective with regards to the number of persons present versus the number of persons killed. Although the body count of Virginia Tech (33) is a staggering number, there were *hundreds* of people present (thousands in the immediate area), and Cho had 400 rounds on his person. Most active shooter events have a similar pattern, which is why there are so many wounded people rather than outright deaths – the shooters just don't have very good aim. This is mainly due to the pressure of the event, and the shooter's adrenaline, which degrades the fine motor skills required to accurately fire a weapon. Even trained recreational shooters who spend a lot of time at the range will have difficulty shooting at moving targets such as fleeing persons. This mainly because the training for such a contingency is hard to come by: One would need to have previous combat experience in actually shooting moving targets (none of the above examples had this), or spend time training with moving targets (paintball, simunitions). Fixed target training alone does not develop the skills necessary to reliably engage moving targets. This works in your favor, as will be discussed in the section on what you can do to avoid being a victim.

Contained area: Most active shooter events occur within a contained area where egress of the victims is impeded due to the layout of the building. People running away down a hallway, for example, as in the Columbine massacre, are funneled by the geography of the hallway into convenient groups. One doesn't need to be much of a marksman to fire down a hallway and hit people. Additionally, the shooter will often try to lock himself into the premises, such as Cho, who chained the doors shut. The idea is to use the building(s) as a containment area for victims. Not all active shooters take place within buildings, however. Jared Loughner shot many victims outside of a Tucson supermarket – in the open air – as they were gathered to hear Congresswoman Gabrielle Giffords speak, leading us to our next point;

Target rich environment: A contained area is no good if adequate targets aren't present. Active shooters who are motivated by body count alone will seek out a target rich environment, and will plan two things carefully: 1) An appropriate venue with a sufficient number of victims, and 2) the appropriate time of day. Cho shot up Virginia Tech when the students were all conveniently in their classrooms. Loughner waited

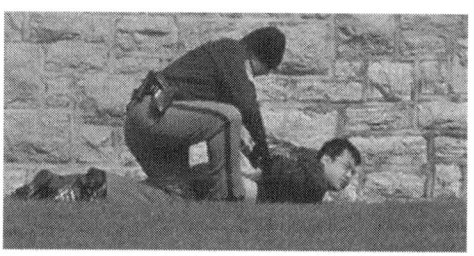

until Congresswoman Giffords' crowd had assembled to hear her speak. Holmes waited until the theater was full of moviegoers and the film was well underway before shooting. Hennard waited for the lunch time crowd to get into full swing before attacking Luby's. The point is, active shooters seek a target rich environment and choose the time and place for maximum effect.

Gun free zone: While the topic of gun control is beyond the scope of this manual, realize that active shooters will typically perform their shootings in an area with strict gun control. Realize that in all of the examples of active shooter incidents cited in this work, *all of them* were perpetrated in areas where either a) the personal possession of firearms was expressly prohibited by law or policy, and b) concealed carry by the citizenry was illegal. There is a critical point to be realized here: *active shooters never, ever plan for any armed resistance, because they know there won't be any.* The significance of this point cannot be understated. Active shooters usually plan suicide as the culmination of their rampage, so they aren't afraid of dying per se, but they do want to accomplish their goal of killing the maximum number of people possible, and armed resistance gets in the way of that goal. Also, most active shooters are aware that by the time police arrive, they will have killed a significant number of people, so it's safe to say that police presence, unless it happens to be already *within* the area they are planning to raid, *is not a factor for an active shooter!*

Weapons used: Contrary to public misconception, most active shooters mainly use commonly available handguns, shotguns, and rifles to perpetrate their attacks. There hasn't been a single case of an active shooter using a machine gun or any other automatic, restricted, or military weapon to carry out an attack. Active shooters overwhelmingly use what is commercially available.

A PROFILE DEVELOPS

Taking the above points in mind, a profile emerges of a typical active shooter incident (if any of them can be called typical):

A single shooter, armed with commercially available weaponry, will strike a target rich, contained environment. He will extensively plan for the attack, and will strike an area where he is certain that he won't meet any significant armed resistance. He will usually not plan to survive the encounter.

The above statement is staggering in its assessment and brevity, but we can use it to formulate a strategy to survive such an attack. Knowing the enemy and his tactics is key to surviving the encounter.

WHAT THE POLICE WILL DO

Before you ask yourself what you would do, it would be nice to know what the police plan on doing. We are fortunate enough to live in a country which has rapid police response to almost any incident. Our policemen are highly trained and arrive with the finest and most technologically advanced equipment. The problem is, however, for decades, the only police response to an active shooter was to simply *wait the event out*.

Recall that in the case of Huberty, who gunned down innocents at the San Ysidro McDonalds, he had a mind boggling *77 minutes* to kill people. It's a staggering  and shocking amount of time, and the results spoke for themselves. The police *gave* him that time due to their training. Before you go up in arms, realize what police doctrine was for the better part of the 20th century:

- Upon learning of an active shooter, the responding officer would call in the incident, and await backup.
- Backup would arrive, and a protective cordon was laid in a 360 degree perimeter to the facility. The cordon was to ensure that the suspect did not escape.
- Police management would be called in, often with a hostage negotiator in tow.
- The SWAT team would arrive, and augment the positions of the first responders; they would set up viewing and shooting positions

on nearby rooftops and radio the actions of the shooter(s) back to higher headquarters.

- If the shooter proved incommunicative or violent, the SWAT team was ordered to take him out. Oftentimes, this occurred in one of two ways; 1) the shooter would be shot by a sniper (i.e. the way Huberty died), or 2) the building would be stormed by the team.

While all of this sounds like a reasonable, solid plan, it had only one problem: it took time. Lots of time. By the time a perimeter was set up and the SWAT team arrived, you could be looking at half and hour or more. Hostage negotiators would try desperately to make contact with the shooter, but there was a little problem: *the shooter wasn't negotiating!* He didn't want to negotiate! His goal was to kill as many people as rapidly as possible, and police tactics of the time helped him do it. While the cordon was being set up and higher management was being in-

formed of a shooting, the shooter was killing. While the SWAT team was gearing up the shooter was killing. While the negotiators were trying to contact the shooter, the shooter was killing.

It took some time for police doctrine to accept the fact that an active shooter's goal is to simply kill people and then kill himself. No ransom, no demands, no plane ride at the nearest airport, no suitcase full of money. Just wholesale slaughter.

MODERN POLICE RESPONSE TO AN ACTIVE SHOOTER

Thankfully, the old method of policing with regards to an active shooter is dead and buried (pun intended), and a newer, more practical method is in active use nation wide. Currently, if an active shooter incident unfolds, the following will occur:

- The responding officer will arrive on the scene of an active shooter.
- After a rapid assessment of the situation, the officer will usually arm himself with a high powered patrol rifle, which most policemen carry in their patrol cars these days. No longer are police under armed when dealing with a shooter.
- He will make every effort to *immediately* enter the structure by any means available. He is usually equipped with bolt cutters, and sometimes, breaching rounds for his shotgun.
- The officer will charge inside, moving in a tactical fashion *towards* the sound of the gunfire.
- His goal is to immediately make contact with the active shooter and engage the threat.
- His number one priority is speed, and the minimization of loss off life.

This new doctrine has already helped to save much human life. While it does put the individual officer at elevated risk (as opposed to waiting outside until backup arrives), it has more or less been universally accepted that risking the life of an officer or officers versus potentially dozens of innocent victims is a worthy compromise. If in an active shooter situation, you can now expect immediate and direct police assistance by the first responding officers. While they will still set up a perimeter and call the SWAT team, no longer will they wait to make entry and contact the shooter. It's a good compromise that seems to be working well thus far; it most certainly would have prevented the sheer number of victims that the San Ysidro shooting produced.

WHAT YOU NEED TO DO

You are now armed with the knowledge of what an active shooter is after, what sort of targets he will choose, and how he will carry out his wholesale slaughter. You now know what the responding police will do. Now its time to learn about what *you* should do during such a situation.

The first and painfully obvious rule of active shooters is to *not be there when they strike*. For better or worse, some people have just sworn off of visiting the busy, public places favored by active shooters. Places like restaurants, shopping malls, public gatherings, and demonstrations are magnets for active shooters. These target rich environments are the stomping ground of those who desire mass casualties. Whether it's feasible to give up public life is only answerable by you. Living in fear and avoiding public places is not necessarily the answer, but it is a viable choice if you absolutely positively never want to encounter an active shooter.

Okay, so maybe you really don't want to give up public life. No one will blame you; after all, if you give up going out into public the shooters and all of the other boogey men will have won the battle. What can you do to prepare for an active shooter? What can you do to build up some tactical awareness? Here are ten things you can do *right now*, next time you go out, to be prepared:

1. **Keep your back to the wall, cowboy:** This may seem like an old western gunslinger practice, but it is very useful and might just save your life. Where you happen to be during an active shooter scenario is sometimes the difference between life and death. All shooters must use a method of ingress into the building, and this is usually the front door. Whenever you visit a restaurant, public place, or

theater, pick a seat that puts your back to the wall. This relieves you of having to cover your six – one less direction to worry about.

2. **Position yourself so you can see the front door:** If at all possible, with your back to the wall, pick a spot where you can comfortably see the main entrance to wherever you happen to be. Make sure that you only see the door, rather than sitting in the *direct line of fire* to it. Having visual contact on the entryway from a 30-40 degree angle is optimum.

3. **Watch the doors:** Actually watch the people coming through. Learn to observe without staring. See who comes and goes, and what they look like and how they act. Realize that most active shooters *have already been to the place they intend to shoot*. You might just observe one casing the place. If the same guy comes in twice within a short period of time and leaves both times, consider it a warning and stay alert. Might just be innocent, but might not be!

4. **Keep an eye out for open fire exits:** An open fire exit with no alarm sounding should make alarm bells ring in your head! Tell the staff that they have an open door. It could be a maintenance issue, or it could be the method of ingress for an active shooter. Report it!

5. **Do a mental survey of the place:** Note the entrances and exits. Note the back door, if there is one. Keep an eye out for opening windows, and if you are on anything but the ground floor, look out the windows and see what is below. Many people have jumped out

of windows during active shooters and have either plunged to their deaths or gotten badly injured. Know what's there.

6. **Look for heavy objects that can be used as improvised weapons:** This could be a brick, heavy sugar shaker, a broom handle – anything. The active shooter will not be expecting any serious resistance. Be prepared to provide some!

7. **Always have a method of communication:** And be prepared to use it! During the Aurora Theater shooting, many people texted and tweeted the fact that there was an active shooter rather than phoning the police! Make sure you have a cell handy, and when in doubt, call 911 immediately!

8. **Carry a backup weapon allowed by local law:** Whether you are allowed to carry a handgun, pocket knife, pepper spray, or what have you, carry it. Realize that some resistance is better than no resistance. Remember, you don't necessarily need to have these to engage the shooter. Even if you have a handgun on your person, simply using it to shoot out a plate glass window and escaping is better than nothing.

9. **Be an observer of people:** Look at people, actually look at them rather than being oblivious. Look for signs of nervousness or the look of a thousand yard stare. Look for signs of intoxication or drug use. Dilated pupils and profuse sweating on a cool day is a sure sign of trouble to come.

10. **Be prepared to act:** Most victims will simply sit there and await their fate. Temporary paralysis when confronted with a grave threat is normal, but it should pass quickly. Act immediately, and realize that even momentarily remaining stationary could mean death. Act. Run. Engage. Alert someone. The key here is to *do something*, not freeze.

IT'S TOO LATE

Someone is in the building you're in, and they're shooting. You hear gunshots – something is definitely amiss. Assuming you are not the first one to make contact with an active shooter, you have a precious few moments to figure out what you want to do. ACT NOW BEFORE IT'S TOO LATE!

So what do you do when the threat is real? What can you possibly do to avert this situation and come out alive? Here are ten tactics that you can use, ten things to keep in the back of your head during an active shooter incident:

1. **Escape:** If you remember one thing and one thing only, remember this. Escape, plain and simple. Many active shooter deaths have come about because people were trying to do something other than trying to escape. Like what? How about like trying to help others, trying to find a hiding spot, or trying to barricade a door. When you have the opportunity to escape, you must take it. Escape to the outside deflates the one weapon that the active shooter has against you – *containment*. You are no longer trapped inside a small room or corridor. You are a harder target to hit when running away. Escape becomes more complicated when you have loved ones or friends with you. Urge them to do the same – the natural human reaction is to cower and hide, but fight the urge to do so and put escape first on your list.

2. **Don't run in a straight line:** If you make a break for it, the worst thing you can do is to run in a dead straight line in front of the shooter. Running in a straight line makes you an easy target – zig zag instead. It's has already been proven that due to adrenaline, the shooter's fine motor skills will be degraded, and he needs those skills in order to shoot you while running in a zig zag pattern.

3. **Make an escape where there is none:** Bust out a window and jump, if you can. Smash through the drywall and get into an adjacent room. Crawl up into the drop ceiling. Now is the time to think unconventionally – you need to outsmart the shooter. What if you're too high up and can't jump out of the window? Consider breaking it anyways, then hiding in the room somewhere. The shooter might just think you actually did jump and move on to the next room.

4. **Erect a barricade:** If you're in a windowless room or are way too high up to consider going out the window, erect a barricade to block the door. Use everything at your disposal here, but *build it quick* and *get out of the way!* Many people have been shot trying to physically block the door, or while standing just behind the barricade. The shooter will often shoot right through the door in anger – don't be standing behind the door. Let the barricade block it for you.

5. **Never lie flat on the ground to avoid gunfire:** If someone is shooting, the best position to be in is crouched down low, balancing on one or two feet, with your arms around your knees. You want as little of your body touching the floor as possible. This is because *bullets travel along floors!* A bullet that is shot down low will hit the floor, bounce off, and travel parallel to the floor, a few inches above it, until it runs out of energy and strikes something. That something could be you, lying flat on the ground! Stay off the floors!

6. **Keep off the walls:** As stated above, bullets are funneled by floors. They are also funneled by walls. If someone shoots down a hallway, the bullet might impact the wall, bounce, and travel parallel to the wall only a few inches off of it. Stay off the walls!

7. **Do not attempt to engage the shooter:** Unless you are a peace

officer or highly trained, your mission is to escape, hide, or barricade. It is not to engage, unless a spectacular opportunity presents itself. Put as much distance between you and the shooter as possible.

8. **Hide:** This one is a mixed bag. Make sure your hiding spot is a good one and you will not easily be spotted. The human psyche has a tendency to introduce wishful thinking into a high stress situation. People will often hide under desks and other furniture where they are clearly visible in an almost ridiculous manner, and then be shot. If you have to hide, make sure your hiding spot is a good one, and preferably, behind a barricade.

9. **Stay alert even after the shooter has passed:** Keep in mind that in many active shooter cases, the shooter has gone room to room, killing as he goes. But in a sickening and cruel twist, the shooter will often return to rooms he previously was in, shooting again. If you are hidden, stay hidden until the police arrive! Don't make the mistake of getting complacent – realize the shooter can and often does return. Keep your barricade up and stay under cover until the police arrive.

10. **Improvise a weapon:** If contact with the shooter seems likely, you need to improvise a weapon, and fast. Normally, you'll do everything you can to not engage the shooter. Escape, hiding, and barricades are always best, but if you find yourself cornered with no chance for escape or hiding, you must act. The shooter will not usually expect resistance – if he did, he wouldn't undertake this rampage. Almost anything can be used as a weapon! Pick something up, and strike, going for the face and the weapon hand. If you are about to die, it's best to go out fighting rather than cowering – you might just surprise yourself and save the day, as most shooters simply don't have a contingency plan for any sort of resistance.

QUESTIONABLE TACTICS

There are some tactics that have worked for some people, but not for others, and therefore they really aren't viable. If a given tactic works only *half* the time, it doesn't make sense to use it *all* the time. There are many stories of survival from horrendous active shooter incidents in which people have survived through questionable means, but that doesn't mean you need to try these things. Here are a couple:

Playing dead: The jury is still out on this one. In the San Ysidro shooting of 1984, at least one individual survived by playing dead. Same thing goes for the Columbine Massacre; one teenager happened to find himself behind two dead bodies and he was covered in their blood. The assailants passed him by. On the other hand, there are countless examples of active shooters making sure the people are dead by shooting them execution style as they lay there. This is really tragic, because the people were alive and well up until the point where the shooter ended their lives. Playing dead is a passive resistance tactic that may or may not work, and is probably only good for the old and infirm who don't have any other options. Remember, playing dead is a form of doing *nothing*. These could be your last moments on earth. Do you really want to spend them doing nothing, or do you want to go out running, fighting, or something else more active?

Begging for your life: Begging for your life or otherwise attempting to reason with the shooter has also worked in some cases, but not in others. Anders Breivik, the Norway shooter that killed 77 people, let some individuals go after questioning them. The Columbine perpetrators did the same. In other cases, however, the active shooter attempted to question the victims, but shot them anyways. Seung-Hui Cho, the Virginia Tech shooter, called out many taunts to his victims, some of which attempted to answer or reason with him. He shot them anyways. The bottom line here is to not have any contact with the shooter or engage him in any way. These are people who have lost all sense of reason; they are past the point of listening to rational arguments or pleas for life. If you must do something out of necessity and lack of other options, attack them with all the ferocity you have.

IN CLOSING

An active shooter scenario is perhaps the most shocking and scary thing that could ever happen to you in your life. Nothing you do, no amount of planning, will make it any less scary. Experiencing the feeling of fear is not a weakness, however. Realize that you can still be scared and make good tactical decisions. You don't need to be a victim or remain paralyzed – you can act right now, and save yourself and your family while others cower and beg for their lives. Being a survivor is a state of mind, and ethos. The sooner you embrace that, the better off you'll be.